The Life Cycle of the Orca

Written by Moira Butterfield

T0317869

Contents

Meet the orcas	2
The birth of an orca	6
Life as a young orca	16
Becoming a hunter	30
Growing up	40
Life and death	44
Glossary	52
Index	53
The life of an orca	54

Collins

Meet the orcas

Orcas are a type of dolphin, the largest of all dolphin **species**. Adult orcas grow to between 7 metres and 9.7 metres long – almost the length of a school bus! The males are heavier than the females and can weigh six tonnes or more. The heaviest ever recorded was a whopping ten tonnes.

Orcas are cetaceans, the name given to a family of animals that includes dolphins and whales. All cetaceans are mammals, a category of creatures that give birth to live babies and make milk to feed their newborns. All mammals breathe air – orcas have a **blowhole** on the top of their head to do this. Orcas are family-focused and stay living with their relatives all their lives, in a group called a pod.

Orcas swim in pods of 5 to 50 creatures.

Despite being a dolphin species, orcas are also known as killer whales. Sailors gave them this name because they noticed what powerful hunters they were. When working together, orcas are able to kill and eat whales much larger than themselves, and they can even kill such dangerous creatures as great white sharks. Like all dolphins, orcas are carnivores, eating only meat.

Orca size comparison

school bus (14 m)

human diver (1.8 m)

male orca (up to 9.7 m)

Orcas are found in all the world's oceans but they particularly seem to like cooler waters and coastal areas. They live in the greatest numbers in the Pacific Ocean (in the Gulf of Alaska), the North Atlantic Ocean (especially off the coast of Norway) and in the Southern Ocean around Antarctica.

Nobody knows exactly how many orcas there are in the wild, though it's thought there might be around 50,000. We do know that there are 50–60 orcas kept in captivity in theme parks around the world.

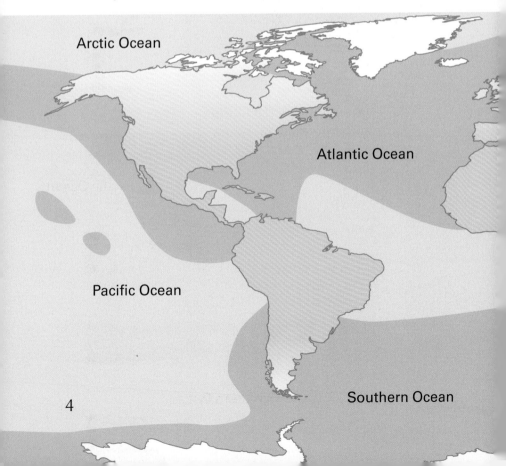

Arctic Ocean

Atlantic Ocean

Pacific Ocean

Southern Ocean

It's very controversial to keep orcas in captivity because captive orcas are forced to live very differently from those in the wild, in small pools without their pods around them. Campaigners are trying to cut down the number.

Arctic Ocean

Key:

where whales are found in the greatest numbers

Pacific Ocean

Indian Ocean

Southern Ocean

5

The birth of an orca

Orcas only mate with orcas from other pods, never their own, because orcas in the same pod are members of the same family.

Pods sometimes meet up, and that's when mating takes place. The pods then separate and go their own way, so the father of an orca calf is never around when it's born.

Orca Stat Orcas aren't ready to breed until they are around 12 years old. By then, the males will have grown to about 6.7 metres long and the females to about 4.9 metres long.

The moment an orca calf is born underwater.

Female orcas are pregnant for around 17 months and, while orcas are born all year round, more are born in winter than in summer.

In-between their pregnancies, females look after their **offspring**. A female wouldn't normally have a new calf until her previous calf is around three to five years old and big enough to look after itself. A female orca has around four to six calves during her lifetime.

The other orcas in a pod help mothers to look after their calves.

Babies in captivity

Orca breeding in captivity
is very controversial.
Campaigners against
keeping orcas in theme
parks say that the females
often give birth when
they're too young.
Wild orcas live with their
mothers all their life, but
in theme parks they're
sometimes separated.

Baby orcas are born underwater. They usually emerge tail first, though occasionally they are born head first. A newborn orca will **instinctively** swim to the surface to take its first breath, helped by its mother.

The white markings on a baby calf look slightly yellow at first. The skin turns whiter as the calf grows. Calves are born with a soft and floppy dorsal (back) fin and tail, but these will gradually stiffen up.

Orca Stat Newborns are around 2.6 metres long and weigh about 160 kilograms.

newborn orca (2.6 m)

human diver (1.8 m)

family car (4.6 m)

A newborn orca takes its first breath as soon as it is born.

Calves drink their mother's milk within a few hours of being born and they'll carry on **nursing** for about a year. An orca mother's milk is very rich in fat, helping the baby to grow quickly and develop a thick layer of blubber under its skin. Blubber is fat which helps to keep an orca warm in cold seawater.

Orca Stat A fully-grown orca's blubber layer is 7 to 10 centimetres thick.

A calf feeds underwater by swimming next to its mother as she gently glides along. A newborn feeds several times an hour, 24 hours a day. As it grows, it gets better at sucking milk from its mother, and doesn't need to feed so often.

A one-month-old calf sticks close to its mother.

Orca Stat In their first year, calves grow about 65 centimetres and put on around 400 kilograms.

An orca calf swims slightly behind its mother, in her **slipstream**, because it takes less effort to swim there. The slipstream gives the orca an easy ride!

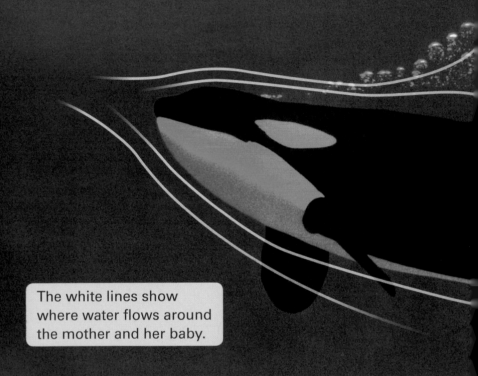

The white lines show where water flows around the mother and her baby.

Orcas usually rest occasionally through the day by staying motionless in the water. But new mothers don't. They keep on swimming for the first month or so, without any sleep, and only begin to rest again as the calf grows. Experts believe this is because a newborn calf doesn't have enough blubber to float or stay warm when it is motionless.

Around half of all newborn orcas don't survive their first year, although we don't know exactly why this is. There's no evidence of babies being attacked by other creatures, but orcas are prone to viruses and infections, and newborns may not be strong enough to survive falling ill.

Life as a young orca

Orcas live in family pods all their lives, so young orca calves grow up with their mothers, grandmothers, sisters, brothers and uncles. The largest pods can include more than 50 orcas. All the orcas help care for the newborns, protecting and teaching them as they grow.

Orca pods that live close to each other and behave in a similar way sometimes meet up, and we call this bigger group a clan. The pods within a clan have similar calls to each other, just like humans living in a particular area might speak with a local accent. Calves start to learn the calls of their pod at five months old, and eventually learn their clan's calls, too.

Some clans of orcas look and behave very differently to each other. For example, off the coast of Alaska, there are clans of orcas that mainly eat salmon, clans that hunt other mammals such as seals, and clans that prefer to eat sharks. These orca clans vary in size and have differing light and dark patches on their skin.

A newborn calf will learn to behave as its pod behaves, whether that's staying in one place to catch fish or making long journeys to catch mammals.

Orca pods vary in whether they stay in one place or travel around.

resident pods	stay in one small area	feed on fish and live in a location where there are lots of fish to catch
transient pods	travel widely	hunt mammals such as seals, dolphins and small whales
offshore pods	live in **open water**	feed mainly on sharks

This orca, which belongs to a transient pod, has just caught a porpoise off the coast of British Columbia.

Early care

Young females spend time with the mothers and calves in their pod, learning how to nurse and look after young orcas. When it's time for them to have their own babies, they'll have the skills they need to be good mothers. As calves grow, they're sometimes looked after by older relatives too, swimming for a while with an uncle, aunt or grandmother in their pod.

If a calf behaves badly, it'll get told off by its relatives. It might be corralled, which means it's forced to stay in one small area for a while, or raked, where its skin is lightly scratched by another orca's teeth.

Sperm whales, bottlenose dolphins and pilot whales also gather in pods. Unlike killer whales, the sperm whales found in pods are not all related to each other but they do help to look after each other's young. A female sperm whale might care for up to four calves while their mothers leave to hunt for food. Bottlenose dolphin pods also aren't all related, and individuals sometimes swap between different pods, but females often come back to their mother's pod to give birth.

Pilot whales stay in family groups, but join together with others to create a school of more than a hundred.

An illustration of a calf being looked after by other pod members.

Orca language

Orca pods communicate with each other using calls, which include whistles, pulsed calls (repeated bursts of sound), popping sounds, jaw-claps and clicks. A young orca makes its first proper call when it's around two months old. Before that, it only makes a high-pitched loud scream to call its mother. When it's about five months old, it starts learning the calls of the pod by copying its mother.

Orcas make noises by blowing air through nasal passages connected to their blowhole, the breathing hole on top of their head. They tend to use whistles for close-up chat and pulsed calls to talk to their group.

Orcas make calling noises using the breathing tubes connected to their blowhole.

No two orca pods use exactly the same selection of calls, though pods that live near to each other will use many that are the same. Pods living widely apart will have completely different calls.

The loudest callers in the ocean are the biggest whales – the blue whales and humpbacks. Their sounds can travel over 3,000 kilometres underwater!

Sound underwater

Sound travels underwater, so orcas can hear each other's calls. We can use an underwater microphone called a hydrophone to hear them, too.

orca   sound waves

hydrophone

Scientists found that a pod living near Iceland had 24 calls, and a pod living near Norway had 23 calls, but none of their calls were the same.

As well as using calls, orcas communicate with body language. They might slap their tails or their pectoral (side) fins on the surface of the water, or even head-butt or snap their jaws if they are irritated. A young calf will soon learn the signals and what they mean, especially if it starts annoying one of its relatives and gets head-butted!

Some orca pods have a special way of greeting each other when they meet, traditions which are passed down from mothers to children. The pods around Vancouver Island, Canada, line up in two rows and then swim in together, tumbling and playing.

When pods that know each other meet, they use the same calls and body language to communicate. Calves soon get to know their neighbours.

Orcas sometimes signal to each other by slapping their tails.

23

Swimming

An orca uses the two parts of its tail, called flukes, to help it swim, moving them up and down. It uses its fins and flukes to help steer in the water by moving their positions to change direction or to stop.

As a calf grows, it gets stronger and faster at swimming. Fully-grown orcas can reach speeds of up to 55 kilometres per hour in short bursts. An orca's pointed body shape and smooth skin helps it slip through the water easily.

Who's fastest?

Although sailfish are the fastest creatures in the ocean, orcas aren't too far behind.

Creature	Kilometres per hour (kph)
sailfish	109
orca	55
common dolphin	38
leatherback turtle	35
fastest human swimmer	7.5

Diving

Young orcas can't dive very far, but as their lungs grow they get better at it. A fully-grown orca can dive 100–200 metres deep for a couple of minutes.

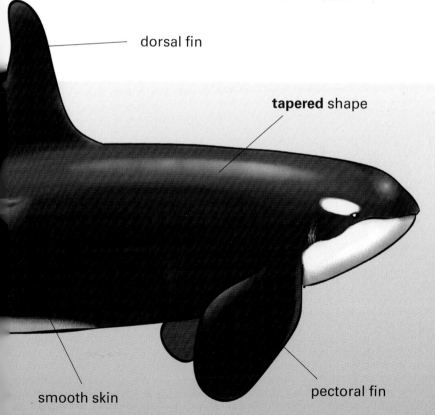

dorsal fin

tapered shape

smooth skin

pectoral fin

Playing

Wild orcas love to play, and it's thought their games help calves to learn the skills they'll need for hunting. Pods like to play games of fish-catch, tossing fish between them. They play a version of tag too, taking it in turns to chase each other.

Swimming tricks

A calf learns various swimming tricks as it grows, and gets stronger by copying the other orcas in its pod.

They jump out of the water, called breaching, and this makes a big splash. The splash makes a loud sound so it could be a signal to other orcas, but nobody knows for sure. It's probably often done purely for fun!

breaching

spyhopping

Orcas stick their heads out of the water to take a look around – this is called spyhopping.

They swim in a certain style, called porpoising, where they go above and below the water. This reduces **drag**, so they can swim faster.

porpoising

Capturing orcas

Orcas are very close to the relatives in their pod, just as humans are close to each other in families. So what happens if a young orca is captured and taken into captivity? Many experts believe that the damage done to the orcas is very great, and it's been proved that they live far shorter lives than orcas in the wild. Orcas in captivity also tend to become more aggressive, stressed and unhealthy.

Campaigners want to ban keeping orcas in captivity for entertainment.

A very young orca performing at Seaworld in San Diego, California.

It's usually young orcas that are captured. A pod is targeted and herded together towards nets, using explosives, speedboats and planes to scare them. A young orca cries out for its relatives to rescue it, as it's lifted out of the water in slings. If it survives, it's taken by truck to its new home in an aquarium, where it's forced to live with orcas it doesn't know.

Campaigners say that stealing young orcas from their families is wrong and should be banned.

Becoming a hunter

Orcas work together as a team to trap their prey, and a young orca will join in the hunt as soon as it's strong and skilled enough. It needs to develop some body features, too.

An orca's top surface is darker than its under surface, which means it blends into the darkness of the sea from above and into the bright sunlight from below, helping it to creep up on the food it's hunting.

An orca is hard to see in shadowy water.

An orca tooth is about 7.6 centimetres long.

Orcas have 48–52 conical teeth, but these aren't used to chew their food. Instead, they tear it into smaller chunks.

Just like human babies, orcas don't get their teeth straight away, but they start to appear at around two to five months old. They'll begin to take lumps of solid food from their mother once their first teeth arrive. They won't start catching food such as fish themselves until all their teeth have appeared.

Orca Stat

Two to four months old – grows upper teeth.
Three to five months old – grows lower teeth.
One year old – will be eating up to 27 kilograms of food a day.

Echolocation

Orcas use echolocation to hunt and navigate. We don't know how good newborn orcas are at echolocation, but it's likely that they get better at it as they get older and the body parts they need for echolocation grow bigger.

Toothed whales, dolphins and porpoises all use echolocation underwater to help them navigate and find food.

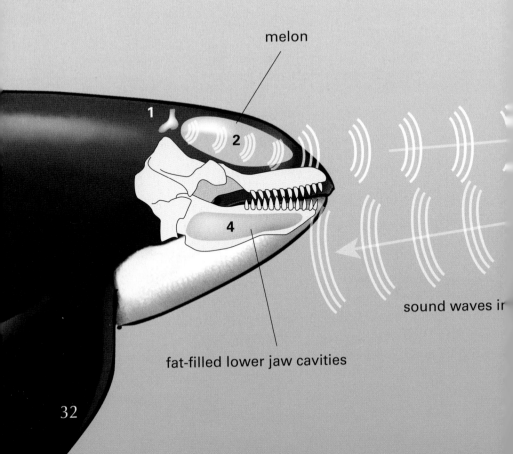

melon

1

2

4

sound waves in

fat-filled lower jaw cavities

How echolocation works

1. An orca makes lots of click noises in rapid succession.
2. The click sounds pass through an area of the forehead called the melon, which changes shape to focus the sound into a beam that projects in front of the orca.
3. The sound beam bounces off any objects in front of the orca.
4. The returning echo passes through fat-filled cavities in the orca's lower jaw and through to the ear, where signals get sent to the orca's brain. Using the signals, the orca can tell the size, shape, direction, speed and distance of the object in front of it.

sound waves out

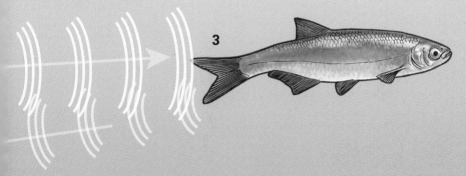

3

Where do orcas hunt?

Resident pods of orcas stay in one area, eating mainly fish and squid. They have learnt where and when to find the tastiest meals, such as off the north coast of North America, where some pods follow the **migration** of salmon.

Transient pods swim a long way to source food, and have learnt the best time to arrive – such as when seals and sea lions are being born in the ocean region where they live.

Orca Stat Orcas eat at least 10% of their own body weight in food every day!

Scientists use harpoons to fire harmless tags into the dorsal fins of orcas. The orcas don't feel the tags, which then track their movements by sending a signal picked up by a **satellite**, and this is how we know where some orcas are.

Orca Stat

One orca pod that was tagged by satellite travelled from Antarctica to Brazil and back in 42 days, swimming 9,400 kilometres non-stop!

Learning to hunt

Orcas teach their youngsters how to hunt. Some of their tactics are very clever.

Along the coast of the Antarctic Peninsula, some orca pods have developed a hunting skill seen nowhere else in the world. Working as a team, they swim towards an ice **floe** where a seal is basking to create a wave that tips the seal into the sea. They'll either catch it to eat, or they'll put the live seal back on to the ice floe to encourage the youngsters in their pod to try it.

One pod of orcas living off Argentina wait for the tide to start coming in and, using precise timing, they deliberately **beach** themselves on a shore full of seals and sea lion pups. They quickly grab a pup before being washed back into the sea by the waves. The older orcas nudge their youngsters on to the beach to encourage them to try the tactic.

36

An adult orca deliberately beaches itself to catch a sea lion off the coast of Argentina.

Hunting techniques

Orcas use different techniques for different prey. When hunting a shark or ray, one section of an orca pod swims in front of it to distract it. Suddenly, another orca speeds in from behind, barging into the shark and quickly flipping it over. Once a shark is upside down, it can't fight back and is easily killed.

Orcas target mother whales and their young by isolating the calf from its mother. The orca pod tires them both out, harrying the pair and even taking bites out of them. Eventually, the mother must abandon her calf to the attackers.

Fish-hunting pods dive around a fish shoal and blow bubbles to herd them tightly together and force them to the surface. Next, one of the orcas slaps its tail beside the shoal, creating a strong sound wave that stuns the fish, giving the orcas an easy mealtime! Other types of dolphins do this fish-herding, too. When the fish are driven together, their tight group is called a bait ball.

This orca herds a shoal of fish in the Arctic Ocean, making an easy mealtime for the gulls too!

Growing up

Males

When a young male orca is around 12–15 years old, his curved dorsal fin begins to grow and straighten out, which is called sprouting. This is a sign that the orca is growing up and will soon be ready to breed. The dorsal fin won't reach its full size until the orca is around 20 years old. By then the fin could be up to 1.8 metres tall – the height of an average man. Female orcas keep their curved, smaller dorsal fins.

As males grow, they start to spend more time with other older males in their pod. Sometimes they team up in a gang of three or four and play intensely, pushing each other and leaping together.

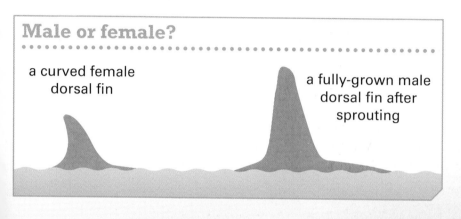

Male or female?

a curved female dorsal fin

a fully-grown male dorsal fin after sprouting

Orca Stat Though males mate outside their pod, they stay with their mothers all their lives, spending at least 40% of their time within a body's length of her.

Females

When females are ready to calve, they start to spend more time away from their mothers, though they usually stay in the pod.

Though young males could start to breed when they are around 10 to 12 years old, females won't usually choose them as mates until they're fully grown – around 20 years old.

family members stick close to their mothers

Life and death

How long a wild orca lives depends on how healthy its life is. Females live to around 50 years old and males to about 30.

In a large pod of around 50 orcas, on average two to three orcas die each year, and two to three calves are born. But scientists studying orca pods have found that fewer babies are being born and believe man-made threats could be harming orca numbers.

Sea mammal life expectancies

blue whale:	89–90 years
humpback whale:	45–50 years
orca:	30–50 years
bottlenose dolphin:	20 years
harbour porpoise:	15–20 years

Orca Stat Lumi, a Northwestern Pacific orca, lived to the age of 98 and was a great-great-grandmother!

Identifying orcas

Scientists can only tell when orcas are born or die by studying pods and getting to know the animals. They do this by taking a photo of each orca and giving it a name.

Each orca has a patch of lighter skin called a saddle behind its dorsal fin. The shape of the saddle is different for every orca, and helps scientists to identify it.

They also record the size and shape of dorsal fins. Some fins have recognisable nicks or kinks.

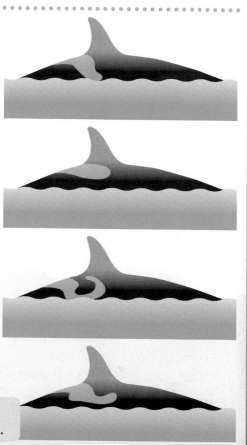

Every orca has its own distinctive saddle shape.

45

Threats

Lack of food is the biggest threat to orca life. In some locations, overfishing may mean there is less food for orcas. Changes on land can also be harmful – for example, if streams where salmon breed get dammed or built on, fewer fish return to the ocean for the orcas to eat.

An atlantic salmon leaping upstream to breed.

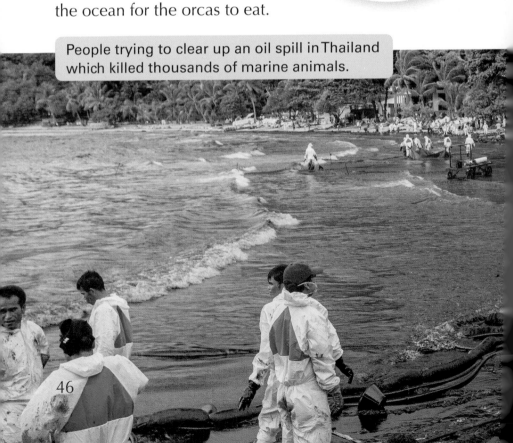

People trying to clear up an oil spill in Thailand which killed thousands of marine animals.

Climate change may lead to fish dying off because of changes in seawater temperature. Oil spillages from ships can also kill off the creatures that orcas eat. A pod off the coast of Alaska fell from 22 orcas to nine after an oil spill killed the seals that the orcas relied on for food.

Increasing sea temperatures caused a rapid increase of algae in the water, which was toxic to these fish.

47

Man-made chemicals that are washed
into the sea can enter the bodies of
animals through what they eat.
One particularly harmful set
of man-made chemicals are
called PCBs, which are linked
to animal ill-health and
fewer babies. PCBs are
especially harmful because
they build up in
an animal's fat and are
never flushed out of
the body. A female orca
will pass PCBs to her
babies through her milk.

When an orca falls
ill, its pod relatives will
try to protect and look
after it. This can mean
a sick orca that wanders
too close to a beach will
lead to other orcas getting
stranded as they try to help it.

PCBs enter the bodies of fish, which are then eaten by creatures such as seals and orcas.

The future of orcas

Advances in technology mean that scientists can discover a lot about orcas and their relatives. They use harmless ultra-thin darts to get skin samples from orcas. The darts bounce off the orcas without them noticing, taking a tiny sliver of skin and blubber. Once the orcas have swum away, the darts are retrieved and tested for **DNA**. Using these DNA records, scientists can identify an orca calf's mother and father.

By learning more about orcas in this way, we can aim to make sure human behaviour doesn't badly affect them, and help orcas to continue breeding successfully in the wild.

Glossary

beach	become stuck on the shore, out of the water
blowhole	a breathing hole on the head of a dolphin or whale
DNA	unique information found in the body cells of every living thing
drag	the force of water pushing against something moving through it
floe	large sheet of floating ice
instinctively	knowing how to do something without having to be taught
migration	a yearly journey completed by some animal species
nursing	drinking a mother's milk
offspring	sons and daughters
open water	a stretch of water far from land
satellite	spacecraft that gathers and sends back information
slipstream	the flow of water behind a fast-moving object
species	a group of living things that share the same characteristics and breed with each other
tapered	a shape that gets narrower and more pointed at the end